Social Security Planning!

Laurel D. Malvern

"Social Security Planning"

Chapter Introduction: Overview of Social Security

Welcome to the first chapter of "Social Security Planning" by Laurel D. Malvern. In this chapter, we'll embark on a journey to understand the cornerstone of financial security for millions of Americans: Social Security.

Social Security is more than just a retirement program; it's a lifeline that provides financial support to retirees, individuals with disabilities, survivors of deceased workers, and their families. Established in 1935 as part of President Franklin D. Roosevelt's New Deal, Social Security has since become one of the most vital social insurance programs in the United States.

At its core, Social Security operates on the principle of intergenerational solidarity. Workers contribute a portion of their earnings throughout their careers, and in return, they're entitled to benefits when they retire or face life's uncertainties. This system not only provides a safety net for individuals and families but also fosters a sense of collective responsibility and support within society.

Throughout this chapter, we'll delve into the fundamentals of Social Security, exploring its history, structure, and key components. We'll discuss how Social Security benefits are calculated, who is eligible to receive them, and the various types of benefits available under the program.

Additionally, we'll address common misconceptions and myths surrounding Social Security, ensuring that readers have a clear understanding of this vital program's purpose and function.

As we navigate through this chapter, I encourage you to approach Social Security with curiosity and an open mind. By gaining a comprehensive understanding of Social Security's role in our lives, you'll be better equipped to make informed decisions about your financial future and maximize the benefits available to you.

So, let's embark on this journey together as we unravel the intricacies of Social Security and lay the groundwork for effective planning and decision-making in the chapters to come.

Warm regards,

Laurel D. Malvern

Chapter: Importance of Social Security Planning

Welcome to the chapter dedicated to understanding the pivotal role of Social Security planning in securing your financial future. In this chapter, we'll explore why Social Security planning is not just beneficial but essential for individuals and families alike.

Social Security serves as a critical foundation for retirement income for millions of Americans. However, relying solely on Social Security benefits may not provide sufficient financial support to maintain your desired standard of living during retirement. That's where strategic planning comes into play.

By engaging in Social Security planning, you can maximize your benefits and optimize your overall retirement income strategy. This process involves careful consideration of factors such as when to claim benefits, how to coordinate benefits with other sources of income, and strategies for maximizing spousal or survivor benefits.

One of the key reasons why Social Security planning is so crucial is its impact on your financial security and longevity in retirement. Making informed decisions about when to start claiming benefits can significantly impact the amount of income you receive throughout your retirement years. By strategically timing your benefit claims, you can potentially increase your lifetime benefits and ensure a more comfortable retirement lifestyle.

Moreover, Social Security planning is not just about maximizing benefits for yourself — it's also about protecting your loved ones' financial well-being. Understanding the various survivor and spousal benefits available under Social Security allows you to make decisions that provide long-term financial security for your family members.

Furthermore, Social Security planning is essential for navigating life's uncertainties, such as disability or premature death. By understanding the disability and survivor benefits offered by Social Security, you can ensure that you and your family are protected in the event of unexpected challenges.

In today's rapidly changing economic landscape and shifting demographics, Social Security planning has never been more critical. As life expectancy increases and retirement becomes more complex, having a solid Social Security plan in place is essential for achieving financial stability and peace of mind.

In the following chapters, we'll delve deeper into the strategies and techniques for effective Social Security planning, empowering you to make informed decisions and secure your financial future.

So, join me as we explore the importance of Social Security planning and unlock the keys to a more secure and prosperous retirement.

Chapter: Budgeting and Money Management

Welcome to the chapter dedicated to mastering budgeting and money management in the context of Social Security planning. In this chapter, we'll explore the fundamental principles of budgeting, how to effectively manage your money, and strategies for optimizing your financial resources to maximize your Social Security benefits.

Budgeting is the foundation of financial success, providing a roadmap for allocating your income and expenses to achieve your financial goals. When it comes to Social Security planning, a well-crafted budget is essential for ensuring that you can meet your financial needs both now and in retirement.

To begin, let's discuss the importance of understanding your current financial situation. Take stock of your income, expenses, assets, and debts to gain clarity on your financial standing. This knowledge will serve as the basis for creating a realistic budget that aligns with your Social Security goals.

Next, we'll explore strategies for creating a budget that maximizes your Social Security benefits. By strategically managing your expenses and identifying areas where you can save money, you can free up more resources to invest in your retirement savings and supplement your Social Security income.

Effective money management goes beyond budgeting—it also involves managing debt and expenses wisely. We'll discuss strategies for reducing debt, such as consolidating high-interest loans and prioritizing debt repayment. Additionally, we'll explore ways to minimize expenses without sacrificing your quality of life, from cutting unnecessary expenses to negotiating lower bills.

Furthermore, we'll delve into strategies for saving and investing to build wealth over time. Whether you're contributing to a retirement account or investing in stocks and bonds, developing a sound savings and investment strategy is essential for achieving your long-term financial goals.

Throughout this chapter, you'll gain practical tips and actionable advice for mastering budgeting and money management in the context of Social Security planning. By taking control of your finances and making strategic decisions, you can optimize your resources to maximize your Social Security benefits and achieve financial security in retirement.

In the following chapters, we'll continue to build on these foundational principles, exploring strategies for retirement planning, understanding Social Security benefits, and navigating the complexities of government policies and business dynamics.

So, let's dive in and unlock the keys to effective budgeting and money management for Social Security planning.

Chapter: Understanding Your Current Financial Situation

Welcome to the chapter dedicated to gaining a deep understanding of your current financial situation—a crucial step in effective Social Security planning. In this chapter, we'll explore the importance of assessing your financial standing, understanding your income and expenses, evaluating your assets and debts, and laying the groundwork for a successful financial future.

To begin, let's emphasize the significance of knowing where you stand financially. Understanding your current financial situation serves as the foundation for making informed decisions about your Social Security benefits, retirement planning, and overall financial well-being.

The first step in understanding your financial situation is to assess your income sources. Take stock of all sources of income, including wages, salaries, investment income, rental income, and any other sources of revenue. Understanding your income streams allows you to gauge your financial stability and identify opportunities for increasing your income over time.

Next, let's turn our attention to your expenses. Take a close look at your spending habits and track your expenses over a specified period, such as a month or a year. Categorize your expenses into essential categories (e.g., housing, food, transportation) and discretionary categories (e.g., entertainment, dining out). This exercise will help you identify areas where you may be overspending and opportunities for reducing expenses to free up more resources for savings and investments.

In addition to assessing your income and expenses, it's essential to evaluate your assets and debts. List all of your assets, including cash savings, retirement accounts, investment portfolios, real estate, and other valuable possessions. Likewise, list all of your debts, such as mortgages, car loans, student loans, credit card debt, and any other outstanding obligations. Understanding your assets and debts allows you to assess your net worth and identify areas where you may need to make adjustments to improve your financial health.

Once you have a clear understanding of your current financial situation, you'll be better equipped to make informed decisions about your Social Security benefits and retirement planning. You'll be able to identify areas where you can optimize your finances, maximize your savings, and make strategic decisions to achieve your long-term financial goals.

In the following chapters, we'll build on this foundation, exploring strategies for budgeting, retirement planning, and optimizing your Social Security benefits. By taking control of your financial situation and making informed decisions, you can set yourself up for financial success and security in retirement.

So, let's dive in and begin the journey toward understanding your current financial situation and unlocking the keys to a brighter financial future.

Chapter: Creating a Budget to Maximize Social Security Benefits

Welcome to the chapter focused on creating a budget specifically tailored to maximize your Social Security benefits. In this chapter, we'll delve into the essential steps and strategies for crafting a budget that optimizes your financial resources, aligns with your Social Security goals, and sets you on the path to financial security in retirement.

Budgeting is the cornerstone of effective financial planning, and when it comes to Social Security, a well-designed budget can make a significant difference in maximizing your benefits. By carefully managing your expenses and allocating your resources strategically, you can ensure that you're making the most of your Social Security income.

To begin, let's start by outlining your sources of income, including your Social Security benefits. Understand how much you'll receive from Social Security each month based on your earnings history and retirement age. Knowing your Social Security income allows you to build your budget around this reliable source of retirement income.

Next, assess your other sources of income, such as pensions, retirement savings, and any additional earnings from part-time work or investments. Take stock of all available resources to get a comprehensive view of your financial situation and potential income streams in retirement.

Once you've identified your sources of income, it's time to analyze your expenses. Categorize your expenses into essential categories (e.g., housing, utilities, groceries, healthcare) and discretionary categories (e.g., entertainment, dining out, travel). Determine how much you're currently spending in each category and identify areas where you can potentially reduce expenses to free up more resources for savings and investments.

As you create your budget, consider how your Social Security benefits fit into your overall retirement income strategy. Explore different claiming strategies, such as delaying benefits to increase your monthly payments or coordinating benefits with a spouse to maximize your combined income. By incorporating these strategies into your budget, you can ensure that you're making the most of your Social Security benefits over the long term.

Throughout the budgeting process, remember to be realistic and flexible. Life circumstances may change, and your budget may need to be adjusted accordingly. Regularly review and update your budget to reflect changes in your income, expenses, and financial goals.

By creating a budget specifically tailored to maximize your Social Security benefits, you can optimize your financial resources, minimize financial stress, and achieve greater security and peace of mind in retirement. In the following chapters, we'll continue to explore strategies for retirement planning, investment management, and navigating the complexities of Social Security to help you achieve your long-term financial goals.

So, let's dive in and begin crafting a budget that sets you on the path to financial success and prosperity in retirement.

Chapter: Managing Debt and Expenses Effectively

Welcome to the chapter dedicated to mastering the art of managing debt and expenses effectively in the context of Social Security planning. In this chapter, we'll explore strategies for reducing debt, minimizing expenses, and optimizing your financial resources to maximize your Social Security benefits and achieve greater financial security.

Debt can be a significant obstacle to financial stability, especially in retirement. High-interest debt, such as credit card debt or personal loans, can eat away at your income and erode your savings over time. Therefore, one of the first steps in effective debt management is to prioritize debt repayment.

Start by listing all of your debts, including outstanding balances, interest rates, and minimum monthly payments. Identify high-interest debts that are costing you the most in interest charges and focus on paying them down first. Consider consolidating high-interest debts into a lower-interest loan or exploring balance transfer options to reduce interest costs and accelerate your debt repayment.

In addition to debt repayment, it's essential to minimize your ongoing expenses to free up more resources for savings and investments. Take a close look at your spending habits and identify areas where you can cut back or eliminate unnecessary expenses. This could involve anything from reducing discretionary spending on dining out or entertainment to renegotiating bills for services like cable, internet, or insurance.

When it comes to managing expenses effectively, small changes can add up to significant savings over time. Consider implementing strategies such as meal planning, buying in bulk, or using coupons to reduce your grocery bill. Look for opportunities to save on recurring expenses by shopping around for better deals or negotiating lower rates with service providers.

Moreover, it's crucial to establish a budget and stick to it to avoid overspending and accumulating more debt. Track your expenses regularly and adjust your budget as needed to stay on track with your financial goals. By living within your means and prioritizing savings and debt repayment, you can achieve greater financial stability and security in retirement.

As you navigate the process of managing debt and expenses effectively, remember to stay focused on your long-term financial goals. By taking proactive steps to reduce debt, minimize expenses, and optimize your financial resources, you can position yourself for success in maximizing your Social Security benefits and achieving greater financial security in retirement.

In the following chapters, we'll continue to explore strategies for retirement planning, investment management, and navigating the complexities of Social Security to help you achieve your financial goals and secure your future.

So, let's dive in and begin mastering the art of managing debt and expenses effectively for Social Security planning.

Chapter: Strategies for Saving and Investing

Welcome to the chapter dedicated to exploring strategies for saving and investing in the context of Social Security planning. In this chapter, we'll delve into the importance of saving for retirement, different types of investment vehicles, and strategies for building wealth over time to complement your Social Security benefits.

Saving for retirement is a critical component of ensuring financial security in your later years. Social Security benefits alone may not provide enough income to maintain your desired standard of living in retirement, so it's essential to supplement your benefits with additional savings and investments.

One of the first steps in saving for retirement is establishing an emergency fund to cover unexpected expenses and financial emergencies. Aim to set aside three to six months' worth of living expenses in a liquid, easily accessible account, such as a high-yield savings account or money market fund.

Once you have an emergency fund in place, focus on contributing to retirement accounts such as employer-sponsored plans (e.g., 401(k), 403(b)) or individual retirement accounts (IRAs). Take advantage of any employer matching contributions to maximize your retirement savings potential and accelerate your wealth-building efforts.

When it comes to investing, diversification is key to managing risk and maximizing returns over the long term. Consider investing in a mix of asset classes, such as stocks, bonds, and real estate, to spread risk and capture potential growth opportunities. Asset allocation should be tailored to your risk tolerance, investment horizon, and financial goals.

For those nearing retirement, it's essential to reassess your investment strategy and adjust your asset allocation accordingly. As you approach retirement age, consider shifting towards a more conservative investment mix to preserve capital and minimize the impact of market volatility on your portfolio.

In addition to traditional retirement accounts, explore other investment options such as taxable brokerage accounts, real estate investments, or alternative assets. Diversifying your investment portfolio can provide additional sources of income and enhance your overall financial security in retirement.

Throughout the saving and investing process, it's crucial to stay disciplined and avoid common pitfalls such as chasing hot investment trends or timing the market. Instead, focus on a long-term investment strategy based on your financial goals and risk tolerance, and stick to your plan through market ups and downs.

By implementing sound saving and investing strategies, you can build wealth over time, complement your Social Security benefits, and achieve greater financial security and peace of mind in retirement. In the following chapters, we'll continue to explore strategies for optimizing your Social Security benefits and navigating the complexities of retirement planning.

So, let's dive in and begin exploring strategies for saving and investing to secure your financial future.

Chapter: Retirement Planning

Welcome to the chapter dedicated to retirement planning—an essential aspect of Social Security planning. In this chapter, we'll explore the importance of retirement planning, strategies for maximizing your Social Security benefits, and steps you can take to achieve financial security and peace of mind in retirement.

Retirement planning is about more than just setting aside money for your later years; it's about envisioning the lifestyle you want in retirement and taking proactive steps to make that vision a reality. Social Security benefits are a critical component of retirement income for many Americans, but they may not be enough to cover all of your expenses in retirement. Therefore, it's essential to supplement your Social Security benefits with additional savings and investments.

One of the first steps in retirement planning is to assess your retirement readiness by estimating your retirement income needs and evaluating your current financial resources. Consider factors such as your desired retirement age, anticipated living expenses, healthcare costs, and expected Social Security benefits. By gaining clarity on your financial goals and resources, you can develop a personalized retirement plan tailored to your unique circumstances.

Next, explore strategies for maximizing your Social Security benefits to optimize your retirement income. Factors such as your claiming age, earnings history, and marital status can impact the amount of Social Security benefits you receive. Consider delaying benefits to increase your monthly payments, coordinating benefits with a spouse to maximize your combined income, or leveraging spousal or survivor benefits to enhance your overall financial security.

In addition to Social Security benefits, explore other sources of retirement income such as employer-sponsored retirement plans, individual retirement accounts (IRAs), pensions, annuities, and investment income. Diversifying your income streams can provide additional sources of financial support and reduce reliance on any single source of income.

As you approach retirement age, revisit your retirement plan regularly and make adjustments as needed to stay on track with your financial goals. Consider factors such as changes in your income, expenses, investment returns, and life circumstances, and adapt your plan accordingly.

Moreover, consider the role of healthcare costs in retirement planning and explore strategies for managing healthcare expenses effectively. Research Medicare eligibility and coverage options, estimate your healthcare costs in retirement, and explore supplemental insurance options to fill any coverage gaps.

By taking proactive steps to plan for retirement, you can achieve greater financial security and peace of mind in your later years. In the following chapters, we'll continue to explore strategies for optimizing your Social Security benefits, managing debt and expenses effectively, and navigating the complexities of retirement planning.

So, let's dive in and begin exploring the ins and outs of retirement planning for Social Security planning.

Chapter: Social Security Retirement Benefits Explained

Welcome to the chapter dedicated to unraveling the intricacies of Social Security retirement benefits. In this chapter, we'll delve into the fundamentals of Social Security retirement benefits, including how they're calculated, when you can start receiving them, and strategies for maximizing your benefits over the long term.

Social Security retirement benefits serve as a foundation of financial support for millions of retirees in the United States. Understanding how these benefits work is essential for making informed decisions about your retirement planning and financial future.

At its core, Social Security retirement benefits are based on your earnings history and the age at which you choose to start receiving benefits. Throughout your working years, you pay Social Security taxes on your earnings, which are used to fund the Social Security system and provide benefits to retirees, disabled individuals, survivors, and their families.

The amount of your Social Security retirement benefit is determined by your average indexed monthly earnings (AIME) over your highest-earning years, known as your "earnings record." The Social Security Administration (SSA) calculates your primary insurance amount (PIA) based on your AIME, which represents the monthly benefit amount you're entitled to receive at full retirement age (FRA).

Your FRA is the age at which you're eligible to receive your full Social Security retirement benefit, which is determined by your year of birth. For most individuals, FRA ranges from 66 to 67 years old. However, you have the option to claim benefits as early as age 62 or delay benefits until as late as age 70.

Claiming benefits before your FRA results in a permanent reduction in your monthly benefit amount, while delaying benefits beyond your FRA results in a permanent increase in your monthly benefit amount. The decision of when to start receiving benefits depends on various factors, including your financial needs, health status, life expectancy, and retirement goals.

In addition to your own retirement benefit, you may be eligible for spousal or survivor benefits based on your spouse's earnings record. Spousal benefits are available to spouses who are at least age 62 and married to a worker who is eligible for Social Security retirement benefits. Survivor benefits are available to widows, widowers, and qualifying dependents of deceased workers.

Throughout this chapter, we'll explore strategies for maximizing your Social Security retirement benefits, including how to optimize your claiming age, coordinate benefits with a spouse, and leverage spousal or survivor benefits to enhance your overall financial security in retirement.

By understanding the ins and outs of Social Security retirement benefits, you can make informed decisions about when to claim benefits and how to maximize your income in retirement. In the following chapters, we'll continue to explore strategies for Social Security planning, retirement planning, and achieving financial security in your later years.

So, let's dive in and begin unraveling the mysteries of Social Security retirement benefits.

Chapter: Determining the Best Age to Claim Social Security

Welcome to the chapter dedicated to helping you determine the best age to claim Social Security benefits—a decision that can have a significant impact on your financial security in retirement. In this chapter, we'll explore factors to consider when deciding when to claim benefits, strategies for optimizing your claiming age, and how to maximize your Social Security income over the long term.

Choosing when to start receiving Social Security benefits is one of the most important decisions you'll make in your retirement planning journey. Your claiming age can significantly affect the amount of your monthly benefit and your overall lifetime benefits, so it's essential to carefully weigh your options and consider the implications of each decision.

One of the primary factors to consider when determining the best age to claim Social Security benefits is your full retirement age (FRA). Your FRA is the age at which you're eligible to receive your full Social Security retirement benefit, which is determined by your year of birth. For most individuals, FRA ranges from 66 to 67 years old.

Claiming benefits before your FRA results in a permanent reduction in your monthly benefit amount, while delaying benefits beyond your FRA results in a permanent increase in your monthly benefit amount. The decision of when to start receiving benefits depends on various factors, including your financial needs, health status, life expectancy, and retirement goals.

Claiming benefits early, at age 62, may be appealing if you need income sooner or if you have health concerns that could affect your life expectancy. However, it's important to understand that claiming benefits early results in a reduced monthly benefit amount, which can have a significant impact on your lifetime benefits, especially if you live longer than average.

On the other hand, delaying benefits beyond your FRA can result in an increased monthly benefit amount, up to a maximum of 8% per year for each year you delay benefits until age 70. Delaying benefits can be advantageous if you're in good health, have longevity in your family history, or want to maximize your Social Security income for yourself or your surviving spouse.

When deciding when to claim Social Security benefits, it's crucial to consider your overall financial situation, including your other sources of retirement income, your savings and investments, and your anticipated living expenses in retirement. Additionally, consult with a financial advisor or Social Security expert to explore personalized claiming strategies tailored to your unique circumstances.

By carefully evaluating your options and considering the implications of each decision, you can determine the best age to claim Social Security benefits and maximize your income in retirement. In the following chapters, we'll continue to explore strategies for Social Security planning, retirement planning, and achieving financial security in your later years.

So, let's dive in and begin navigating the complexities of determining the best age to claim Social Security benefits.

Chapter: Maximizing Social Security Benefits through Spousal and Survivor Benefits

Welcome to the chapter dedicated to exploring how you can maximize your Social Security benefits through spousal and survivor benefits—a valuable aspect of Social Security planning that can significantly enhance your financial security in retirement. In this chapter, we'll delve into the eligibility criteria for spousal and survivor benefits, strategies for optimizing these benefits, and how they can complement your overall retirement income strategy.

Spousal benefits are available to spouses who are at least 62 years old and married to a worker who is eligible for Social Security retirement benefits. Spousal benefits allow a non-working or lower-earning spouse to receive a monthly benefit based on their spouse's earnings record, providing additional financial support in retirement.

The amount of spousal benefits you're entitled to receive is typically equal to 50% of your spouse's full retirement benefit if claimed at your full retirement age (FRA). However, you have the option to claim spousal benefits as early as age 62, although doing so will result in a reduced benefit amount.

To maximize your spousal benefits, consider coordinating your claiming strategy with your spouse's claiming strategy. For example, if your spouse plans to delay claiming benefits to increase their monthly benefit amount, you may choose to claim spousal benefits in the meantime to supplement your income until you're eligible for your own benefits.

Survivor benefits are available to widows, widowers, and qualifying dependents of deceased workers. Survivor benefits provide financial support to individuals who have lost a spouse or parent and can help ensure their continued financial security after a loss.

To qualify for survivor benefits, you must be the widow, widower, or qualifying dependent of a deceased worker who was eligible for Social Security benefits. The amount of survivor benefits you're entitled to receive is based on the earnings record of the deceased worker and your relationship to them.

Similar to spousal benefits, survivor benefits can be maximized by coordinating your claiming strategy with other sources of retirement income. If you're eligible for both survivor benefits and your own retirement benefits, you may choose to claim one type of benefit first and delay claiming the other to maximize your overall Social Security income.

By understanding the eligibility criteria and strategies for optimizing spousal and survivor benefits, you can maximize your Social Security income and enhance your overall financial security in retirement. Consult with a financial advisor or Social Security expert to explore personalized claiming strategies tailored to your unique circumstances and goals.

In the following chapters, we'll continue to explore strategies for Social Security planning, retirement planning, and achieving financial security in your later years.

So, let's dive in and begin harnessing the power of spousal and survivor benefits to maximize your Social Security income.

Chapter: Planning for Healthcare Costs in Retirement

Welcome to the chapter dedicated to addressing one of the most significant concerns in retirement planning: healthcare costs. In this chapter, we'll explore the importance of planning for healthcare expenses in retirement, strategies for managing these costs effectively, and how to ensure that your healthcare needs are adequately covered in your later years.

Healthcare costs can be a significant financial burden in retirement, with expenses often rising as individuals age and require more medical care. It's essential to plan for these expenses proactively to avoid financial strain and ensure that your retirement savings can sustain you throughout your later years.

To begin, let's discuss the various factors that can contribute to healthcare costs in retirement. These may include expenses such as Medicare premiums, deductibles, copayments, prescription drugs, dental care, vision care, long-term care, and other out-of-pocket expenses not covered by insurance.

One of the first steps in planning for healthcare costs in retirement is to familiarize yourself with Medicare, the federal health insurance program for individuals age 65 and older (as well as certain younger individuals with disabilities). Medicare consists of different parts, each covering specific services:

Medicare Part A (Hospital Insurance): Covers inpatient hospital stays, skilled nursing facility care, hospice care, and some home health care.
Medicare Part B (Medical Insurance): Covers outpatient care, doctor's services, preventive services, and durable medical equipment.
Medicare Part D (Prescription Drug Coverage): Covers prescription drugs and helps lower the cost of prescription medications.
Medicare Advantage (Part C): Offers an alternative way to receive Medicare benefits through private insurance plans that contract with Medicare.
Understanding the different parts of Medicare and how they work is essential for making informed decisions about your healthcare coverage in retirement. Consider factors such as your healthcare needs, budget, and preferences when choosing Medicare coverage options.

In addition to Medicare, consider purchasing supplemental insurance coverage, such as a Medicare Supplement Insurance (Medigap) policy or a Medicare Advantage plan, to help fill gaps in coverage and reduce out-of-pocket expenses.

Moreover, explore strategies for managing healthcare costs effectively, such as staying healthy through preventive care, maintaining a healthy lifestyle, and researching healthcare providers and treatment options to find the most cost-effective solutions.

Furthermore, consider setting aside funds in a dedicated healthcare savings account, such as a Health Savings Account (HSA) or a flexible spending account (FSA), to cover anticipated healthcare expenses in retirement. These accounts offer tax advantages and can help you save for healthcare costs while reducing your taxable income.

By planning for healthcare costs in retirement and exploring strategies for managing these expenses effectively, you can ensure that your healthcare needs are adequately covered and protect your financial security in your later years.

In the following chapters, we'll continue to explore strategies for retirement planning, Social Security planning, and achieving financial security in retirement.

So, let's dive in and begin planning for your healthcare needs in retirement.

Chapter: Supplementing Social Security Income with Retirement Savings

Welcome to the chapter dedicated to exploring the importance of supplementing Social Security income with retirement savings. In this chapter, we'll delve into the role of retirement savings in your overall financial plan, strategies for building and managing retirement savings effectively, and how to maximize your income in retirement by integrating savings with Social Security benefits.

While Social Security benefits provide a valuable source of income in retirement, they may not be sufficient to cover all of your expenses, especially if you have higher living standards or face unexpected costs. Therefore, it's essential to supplement your Social Security income with additional retirement savings to ensure a comfortable and financially secure retirement.

To begin, let's discuss the importance of retirement savings in your overall financial plan. Retirement savings serve as a crucial supplement to Social Security benefits, providing you with additional income to cover expenses, maintain your lifestyle, and achieve your financial goals in retirement.

One of the most effective ways to build retirement savings is through employer-sponsored retirement plans, such as 401(k) plans, 403(b) plans, or Thrift Savings Plans (TSP). These plans offer tax advantages and often include employer matching contributions, allowing you to grow your savings faster and maximize your retirement income potential.

Individual retirement accounts (IRAs) are another valuable tool for retirement savings, offering tax-deferred growth and a wide range of investment options. Traditional IRAs allow you to deduct contributions from your taxable income, while Roth IRAs offer tax-free withdrawals in retirement, providing flexibility in managing your tax liability.

When it comes to managing retirement savings, it's essential to establish a diversified investment portfolio tailored to your risk tolerance, investment horizon, and financial goals. Consider investing in a mix of asset classes, such as stocks, bonds, and real estate, to spread risk and capture potential growth opportunities over the long term.

Moreover, regularly review and adjust your investment portfolio as needed to adapt to changing market conditions, economic trends, and your evolving financial situation. Consult with a financial advisor or investment professional to ensure that your retirement savings strategy aligns with your overall financial plan and retirement goals.

By integrating retirement savings with Social Security benefits, you can maximize your income in retirement and achieve greater financial security and peace of mind. Explore strategies for optimizing your retirement savings, such as maximizing contributions, taking advantage of employer matching contributions, and minimizing investment fees and expenses.

In the following chapters, we'll continue to explore strategies for retirement planning, Social Security planning, and achieving financial security in retirement.

So, let's dive in and begin supplementing your Social Security income with retirement savings to secure your financial future.

Chapter: Education and Reference

Welcome to the chapter dedicated to providing education and reference materials on Social Security planning and retirement preparation. In this chapter, we'll explore valuable resources, tools, and educational materials to help you deepen your understanding of Social Security benefits, retirement planning strategies, and financial literacy.

Understanding Social Security and retirement planning can be complex, but having access to reliable educational resources can empower you to make informed decisions about your financial future. Whether you're just starting your career or nearing retirement age, there are plenty of resources available to help you navigate the complexities of Social Security planning.

One of the best places to start your education on Social Security and retirement planning is the official website of the Social Security Administration (SSA). The SSA website offers a wealth of information on topics such as eligibility requirements, benefit calculation, claiming strategies, and online tools for estimating benefits and planning for retirement.

In addition to the SSA website, there are many reputable books, articles, and online resources available to help you learn more about Social Security planning and retirement preparation. Look for books written by financial experts, retirement planners, and Social Security specialists that provide practical advice and strategies for optimizing your benefits and achieving financial security in retirement.

Furthermore, consider taking advantage of educational workshops, seminars, and webinars offered by financial institutions, retirement planning organizations, and community centers. These events often cover topics such as Social Security claiming strategies, retirement income planning, investment management, and healthcare in retirement.

Online calculators and tools can also be valuable resources for planning and decision-making. Use retirement calculators to estimate your Social Security benefits, determine your retirement income needs, and evaluate different claiming strategies based on your individual circumstances.

Moreover, seek out professional guidance from financial advisors, retirement planners, and Social Security experts who can provide personalized advice and recommendations tailored to your specific financial situation and goals. A qualified advisor can help you develop a comprehensive retirement plan, optimize your Social Security benefits, and navigate the complexities of retirement planning with confidence.

By investing time in education and reference materials on Social Security planning and retirement preparation, you can gain the knowledge and skills needed to make informed decisions about your financial future. Whether you're planning for retirement, optimizing your benefits, or managing your investments, access to reliable resources is essential for achieving financial security and peace of mind in your later years.

In the following chapters, we'll continue to explore strategies for Social Security planning, retirement planning, and achieving financial security in retirement.

So, let's dive in and begin your journey toward greater financial literacy and empowerment in Social Security planning.

Chapter: Explaining Social Security Terminology and Concepts

Welcome to the chapter dedicated to unraveling the terminology and concepts surrounding Social Security. In this chapter, we'll explore key terms and concepts related to Social Security benefits, eligibility, claiming strategies, and more. Understanding these terms is essential for making informed decisions about your Social Security benefits and retirement planning.

Full Retirement Age (FRA):

Full Retirement Age refers to the age at which you're eligible to receive your full Social Security retirement benefit.
FRA is based on your year of birth and typically ranges from 66 to 67 years old for most individuals.
Primary Insurance Amount (PIA):

The Primary Insurance Amount represents the base monthly benefit amount you're entitled to receive at your Full Retirement Age.

PIA is calculated based on your average indexed monthly earnings (AIME) over your highest-earning years.
Early Retirement Age:

Early Retirement Age refers to the earliest age at which you can start receiving reduced Social Security benefits.
Early Retirement Age is typically age 62, but claiming benefits early results in a permanent reduction in your monthly benefit amount.
Delayed Retirement Credits:

Delayed Retirement Credits refer to the increase in Social Security benefits you can earn by delaying claiming benefits beyond your Full Retirement Age.
For each year you delay benefits beyond your FRA, you can earn up to an 8% increase in your monthly benefit amount until age 70.
Spousal Benefits:

Spousal Benefits are Social Security benefits available to spouses who are at least age 62 and married to a worker who is eligible for Social Security retirement benefits.
Spousal benefits allow a non-working or lower-earning spouse to receive a monthly benefit based on their spouse's earnings record.
Survivor Benefits:

Survivor Benefits are Social Security benefits available to widows, widowers, and qualifying dependents of deceased workers.
Survivor benefits provide financial support to individuals who have lost a spouse or parent and can help ensure their continued financial security after a loss.
Medicare:

Medicare is the federal health insurance program for individuals age 65 and older (as well as certain younger individuals with disabilities).
Medicare consists of different parts, including Part A (Hospital Insurance), Part B (Medical Insurance), Part D (Prescription Drug Coverage), and Medicare Advantage (Part C).
Cost-of-Living Adjustment (COLA):

Cost-of-Living Adjustment refers to the annual increase in Social Security benefits to keep pace with inflation.
COLA is based on changes in the Consumer Price Index for Urban Wage Earners and Clerical Workers (CPI-W) and is designed to help maintain the purchasing power of Social Security benefits over time.
By familiarizing yourself with these key terms and concepts, you can navigate the complexities of Social Security planning with confidence and make informed decisions about your retirement benefits. In the following chapters, we'll continue to explore strategies for optimizing your Social Security benefits, managing retirement savings, and achieving financial security in retirement.

So, let's dive in and begin unraveling the terminology and concepts of Social Security.

Chapter: Resources for Further Learning and Assistance. Case Studies and Real-Life Examples.

Welcome to the final chapter of our comprehensive guide on Social Security planning. In this chapter, we'll provide you with valuable resources for further learning and assistance, along with real-life case studies and examples to illustrate key concepts and strategies discussed throughout the book. Whether you're just beginning your journey into Social Security planning or looking to deepen your understanding, these resources and examples will help you navigate the complexities of retirement preparation with confidence.

Resources for Further Learning and Assistance:

Social Security Administration (SSA) Website:

The official website of the Social Security Administration (SSA) offers a wealth of information, resources, and online tools for understanding Social Security benefits, eligibility requirements, and claiming strategies. Visit www.ssa.gov to access valuable resources, estimate your benefits, and manage your Social Security account online.
Retirement Planning Workshops and Seminars:

Many financial institutions, retirement planning organizations, and community centers offer educational workshops, seminars, and webinars on Social Security planning and retirement preparation. Attend these events to learn from experts, ask questions, and gain valuable insights into optimizing your benefits and achieving financial security in retirement.
Books, Articles, and Online Resources:

Explore a wide range of books, articles, and online resources written by financial experts, retirement planners, and Social Security specialists. Look for reputable sources that provide practical advice, case studies, and strategies for maximizing your Social Security benefits and navigating the complexities of retirement planning.
Financial Advisors and Retirement Planners:

Consider seeking professional guidance from certified financial advisors or retirement planners who specialize in Social Security planning and retirement preparation. A qualified advisor can provide personalized advice, develop a comprehensive retirement plan tailored to your goals, and help you navigate the complexities of Social Security with confidence.
Case Studies and Real-Life Examples:

Max and Sarah:

Max and Sarah are a married couple approaching retirement age. Max plans to claim Social Security benefits at his Full Retirement Age (FRA) to maximize his monthly benefit amount, while Sarah plans to delay benefits until age 70 to earn Delayed Retirement Credits. By coordinating their claiming strategy, Max and Sarah can maximize their combined Social Security income and achieve greater financial security in retirement.

Emily:

Emily is a widow who lost her husband at a young age. As a surviving spouse, Emily is eligible for survivor benefits based on her husband's earnings record. By claiming survivor benefits at her Full Retirement Age (FRA) and delaying her own retirement benefits until age 70, Emily can maximize her total Social Security income and maintain her financial independence in retirement.

James:

James is a self-employed individual who has saved diligently for retirement through a combination of employer-sponsored retirement plans and individual retirement accounts (IRAs). By supplementing his Social Security income with retirement savings, James can achieve his desired retirement lifestyle, cover healthcare expenses, and leave a legacy for future generations.

These case studies and real-life examples illustrate the importance of strategic Social Security planning and retirement preparation in achieving financial security and peace of mind in retirement. By leveraging valuable resources and learning from real-life scenarios, you can optimize your Social Security benefits, manage retirement savings effectively, and secure your financial future for the years ahead.

In closing, remember that Social Security planning is a journey, and the decisions you make today can have a profound impact on your financial well-being in retirement. Take advantage of the resources available to you, seek professional guidance when needed, and empower yourself to make informed decisions about your retirement benefits.

Chapter: Government and Business

Welcome to the chapter dedicated to exploring the relationship between government policies, business practices, and Social Security planning. In this chapter, we'll delve into the role of government programs, regulations, and economic factors in shaping Social Security benefits, retirement planning strategies, and financial security for individuals and businesses alike.

Government Policies and Social Security:

Social Security Administration (SSA):

The Social Security Administration (SSA) oversees the administration of Social Security benefits, including retirement, disability, survivor, and supplemental security income programs.
The SSA plays a crucial role in determining benefit eligibility, processing claims, and providing information and resources to individuals planning for retirement.
Legislative Changes:

Government policymakers regularly enact legislative changes to the Social Security program to address funding challenges, demographic shifts, and evolving societal needs.
Changes to Social Security laws and regulations can impact benefit amounts, claiming strategies, and eligibility requirements for retirees and beneficiaries.
Economic Factors:

Economic factors such as inflation, wage growth, unemployment rates, and economic growth can influence Social Security benefits and retirement planning strategies.
Cost-of-living adjustments (COLA) are made annually to Social Security benefits to help maintain the purchasing power of benefits over time, reflecting changes in the Consumer Price Index for Urban Wage Earners and Clerical Workers (CPI-W).
Business Practices and Retirement Planning:

Employer-Sponsored Retirement Plans:

Many businesses offer employer-sponsored retirement plans, such as 401(k) plans, 403(b) plans, and pensions, to help employees save for retirement.
These plans often include employer matching contributions, tax advantages, and investment options to encourage employee participation and retirement savings.
Financial Wellness Programs:

Some businesses provide financial wellness programs and resources to employees to help them manage their finances, plan for retirement, and optimize their Social Security benefits.
Financial wellness programs may include educational workshops, seminars, online resources, and one-on-one counseling to support employees in achieving their financial goals.

Healthcare Benefits:

Businesses may offer healthcare benefits and insurance coverage to employees as part of their overall compensation package.
Healthcare benefits can help employees manage healthcare costs in retirement, supplement Medicare coverage, and ensure access to quality healthcare services.
Government policies and business practices play a significant role in shaping Social Security planning, retirement preparation, and financial security for individuals and businesses. By staying informed about government programs, legislative changes, and business offerings, you can make informed decisions about your retirement benefits, savings strategies, and overall financial well-being.

In the following chapters, we'll continue to explore strategies for Social Security planning, retirement planning, and achieving financial security in retirement.

So, let's dive in and explore the dynamic interplay between government and business in the realm of Social Security planning.

Chapter: Understanding the Role of the Social Security Administration

Welcome to the chapter dedicated to exploring the vital role of the Social Security Administration (SSA) in administering Social Security benefits and serving millions of Americans. In this chapter, we'll delve into the functions, responsibilities, and services provided by the SSA, as well as how it impacts individuals' lives and retirement planning strategies.

The Social Security Administration (SSA) is a federal agency responsible for administering various social insurance programs, including retirement, disability, survivor, and supplemental security income (SSI) programs. Established in 1935 as part of the Social Security Act, the SSA plays a crucial role in providing financial support to individuals and families in need.

Functions and Responsibilities of the SSA:

Determining Eligibility:

The SSA determines eligibility for Social Security benefits based on factors such as age, work history, disability status, marital status, and income level.
Individuals must meet specific criteria to qualify for benefits, including earning enough work credits and satisfying age and disability requirements.
Processing Claims:

The SSA processes applications for Social Security benefits, including retirement, disability, survivor, and SSI benefits. Applicants can apply for benefits online, by phone, or in person at their local SSA office. The SSA evaluates applications, verifies eligibility, and processes benefit payments to eligible individuals.
Providing Information and Resources:

The SSA provides information and resources to help individuals understand their Social Security benefits, rights, and responsibilities.
The SSA website offers a wealth of information, including benefit calculators, retirement planners, FAQs, and publications on various topics related to Social Security planning and retirement preparation.
Administering Programs:

The SSA administers various Social Security programs, including retirement benefits, disability benefits, survivor benefits, and SSI benefits.
The SSA ensures that eligible individuals receive timely and accurate benefit payments, monitors program integrity, and safeguards against fraud and abuse.
Impact on Individuals and Retirement Planning:

Financial Security in Retirement:

Social Security benefits serve as a critical source of income for millions of retirees, providing financial security and stability in retirement.
Understanding Social Security benefits, eligibility requirements, and claiming strategies is essential for individuals planning for retirement and maximizing their retirement income potential.
Access to Benefits and Services:

The SSA plays a crucial role in ensuring that eligible individuals have access to Social Security benefits and services, regardless of their age, income, or disability status. Through its network of field offices, online services, and toll-free phone lines, the SSA provides assistance and support to individuals applying for benefits, appealing benefit decisions, and managing their benefits over time.
Advocacy and Outreach:

The SSA conducts outreach and education initiatives to raise awareness about Social Security benefits, retirement planning, and financial literacy.
The SSA collaborates with community organizations, advocacy groups, and government agencies to reach underserved populations, provide information and resources, and promote financial security for all Americans.
By understanding the role of the Social Security Administration and the services it provides, individuals can navigate the complexities of Social Security planning with confidence and make informed decisions about their retirement benefits. In the following chapters, we'll continue to explore strategies for Social Security planning, retirement preparation, and achieving financial security in retirement.

So, let's dive in and deepen our understanding of the vital role of the Social Security Administration in supporting individuals and families nationwide.

Chapter: Legislative Updates and Changes Impacting Social Security

Welcome to the chapter dedicated to exploring legislative updates and changes that have impacted Social Security benefits, eligibility criteria, and retirement planning strategies. In this chapter, we'll delve into recent legislative developments, their implications for Social Security recipients and retirees, and how individuals can adapt their retirement plans in response to these changes.

Social Security is a dynamic program subject to legislative changes and updates over time. Policymakers enact reforms to address funding challenges, demographic shifts, economic trends, and evolving societal needs. Understanding these legislative updates is essential for individuals planning for retirement and optimizing their Social Security benefits.

Recent Legislative Updates and Changes:

Cost-of-Living Adjustments (COLA):

Each year, Social Security benefits may be adjusted based on changes in the Consumer Price Index for Urban Wage Earners and Clerical Workers (CPI-W), known as Cost-of-Living Adjustments (COLA).

Legislative updates determine the COLA percentage increase, which aims to help maintain the purchasing power of Social Security benefits over time.

Full Retirement Age (FRA):

Legislative changes have altered the Full Retirement Age (FRA) for individuals born after certain years.

For example, the FRA increased gradually from age 65 to age 67 for individuals born in 1960 or later, affecting the timing and calculation of Social Security benefits for future retirees.

Benefit Calculation Methods:

Legislative updates may modify the methods used to calculate Social Security benefits, such as changes to the Average Indexed Monthly Earnings (AIME) formula or adjustments to benefit reductions for early claiming.

Program Solvency and Funding:

Policymakers address the long-term solvency of the Social Security program by proposing reforms to ensure its financial stability.

Legislative changes may include adjustments to payroll taxes, benefit formulas, retirement ages, or other program parameters to address funding shortfalls and ensure the program's viability for future generations.

Implications for Retirement Planning:

Adjusting Retirement Timelines:

Individuals may need to adjust their retirement timelines in response to changes in the Full Retirement Age (FRA) or benefit calculation methods.
Delaying retirement beyond the FRA or adjusting claiming strategies can help maximize Social Security benefits and mitigate the impact of legislative changes on retirement income.
Evaluating Long-Term Financial Plans:

Legislative updates highlight the importance of regularly reviewing and adjusting long-term financial plans to reflect changes in Social Security benefits and retirement income. Individuals should consider factors such as life expectancy, health status, financial goals, and economic conditions when making retirement planning decisions in light of legislative changes.
Seeking Professional Guidance:

Given the complexity of Social Security laws and regulations, individuals may benefit from seeking professional guidance from financial advisors or retirement planners.
Certified professionals can provide personalized advice, analyze the impact of legislative changes on retirement plans, and develop strategies to optimize Social Security benefits in response to evolving policy landscapes.
By staying informed about legislative updates and changes impacting Social Security, individuals can adapt their retirement plans proactively, maximize their benefits, and achieve greater financial security in retirement. In the following chapters, we'll continue to explore strategies for Social Security planning, retirement preparation, and achieving financial well-being in later years.

So, let's dive in and navigate the dynamic landscape of legislative updates and changes impacting Social Security.

Chapter: Employer-Sponsored Retirement Plans and Social Security

Welcome to the chapter dedicated to exploring the relationship between employer-sponsored retirement plans and Social Security benefits. In this chapter, we'll delve into the role of employer-sponsored retirement plans, such as 401(k) plans, 403(b) plans, and pensions, in complementing Social Security benefits and enhancing retirement income security for individuals.

Employer-sponsored retirement plans play a crucial role in helping individuals save for retirement and supplement their Social Security benefits. These plans offer tax advantages, employer contributions, and investment opportunities to help employees build retirement savings over their working years.

Types of Employer-Sponsored Retirement Plans:

401(k) Plans:

401(k) plans are employer-sponsored retirement plans that allow employees to contribute a portion of their pre-tax earnings to individual retirement accounts.
Employers may offer matching contributions or profit-sharing contributions to incentivize employee participation and retirement savings.
403(b) Plans:

403(b) plans are retirement plans offered by public schools, nonprofit organizations, and certain other tax-exempt employers.
Similar to 401(k) plans, 403(b) plans allow employees to make pre-tax contributions to individual accounts, often with employer contributions or matching contributions.
Pensions:

Pensions, also known as defined benefit plans, provide retirees with a fixed monthly benefit based on salary, years of service, and other factors.
Employers fund and manage pension plans, guaranteeing retirees a steady stream of income in retirement, in addition to Social Security benefits.
Role of Employer-Sponsored Retirement Plans in Retirement Planning:

Supplementing Social Security Benefits:

Employer-sponsored retirement plans supplement Social Security benefits by providing additional sources of retirement income.

Contributions to these plans, along with employer matching contributions or contributions, can help individuals build retirement savings and achieve financial security in retirement.

Tax Advantages:

Contributions to employer-sponsored retirement plans are typically made on a pre-tax basis, reducing individuals' taxable income and deferring taxes on investment earnings until retirement.

Tax-deferred growth allows retirement savings to accumulate faster and maximize the value of retirement assets over time.

Diversification of Retirement Income:

Employer-sponsored retirement plans offer investment options that allow individuals to diversify their retirement income sources and mitigate investment risk.

By combining Social Security benefits with retirement savings from employer-sponsored plans, individuals can create a diversified portfolio of retirement income to support their financial needs in retirement.

Maximizing Retirement Income through Integration with Social Security:

Coordinating Claiming Strategies:

Individuals can coordinate their claiming strategies for Social Security benefits and employer-sponsored retirement plans to optimize their retirement income.

Delaying Social Security benefits while contributing to retirement plans can increase overall retirement income and provide greater financial security in later years.

Taking Advantage of Employer Contributions:

Individuals should take full advantage of employer contributions or matching contributions to retirement plans, maximizing their retirement savings potential and leveraging employer-sponsored benefits to supplement Social Security income.
Seeking Professional Guidance:

Given the complexity of retirement planning and Social Security rules, individuals may benefit from seeking professional guidance from financial advisors or retirement planners.
Certified professionals can provide personalized advice, analyze retirement income needs, and develop strategies to integrate Social Security benefits with employer-sponsored retirement plans effectively.
By understanding the role of employer-sponsored retirement plans in retirement planning and integrating them with Social Security benefits, individuals can maximize their retirement income potential, achieve financial security, and enjoy a comfortable retirement lifestyle. In the following chapters, we'll continue to explore strategies for Social Security planning, retirement preparation, and achieving financial well-being in later years.

So, let's dive in and harness the power of employer-sponsored retirement plans to enhance your retirement income security.

Chapter: Public Affairs and Policy

Welcome to the chapter dedicated to exploring the intersection of public affairs and policy with Social Security planning. In this chapter, we'll delve into the broader societal, political, and policy considerations that shape Social Security benefits, retirement planning strategies, and the overall landscape of retirement security for individuals and families.

Social Security is not only a financial safety net for retirees but also a cornerstone of public policy aimed at promoting economic security, reducing poverty among the elderly, and ensuring a dignified retirement for all Americans. As such, public affairs and policy play a significant role in shaping the future of Social Security and retirement planning in the United States.

Key Public Affairs and Policy Considerations:

Demographic Trends:

Demographic shifts, such as aging populations, declining
birth rates, and longer life expectancies, have profound
implications for Social Security financing and sustainability.
Policymakers must consider how demographic changes
impact benefit expenditures, revenue generation, and the
overall solvency of the Social Security program.
Economic Conditions:

Economic factors, including economic growth, inflation,
unemployment rates, and wage trends, influence Social
Security revenues, benefit levels, and cost-of-living
adjustments (COLA).
Policymakers must address economic challenges and
uncertainties to ensure the long-term viability and stability of
the Social Security program.
Legislative Reforms:

Legislative reforms to the Social Security program can have
far-reaching implications for benefit eligibility, retirement
ages, contribution rates, and program financing.
Policymakers debate various reform proposals, such as raising
the retirement age, adjusting benefit formulas, increasing
payroll taxes, or implementing means-testing, to address
funding shortfalls and strengthen the program's financial
sustainability.
Social Security Financing:

The financing of Social Security benefits relies primarily on
payroll taxes collected from current workers to pay benefits to
current retirees.
Policymakers must address funding challenges, such as
demographic shifts, rising healthcare costs, and economic
uncertainties, to ensure the adequacy and reliability of Social
Security benefits for future generations.
Public Perception and Awareness:

Public perception and awareness of Social Security issues influence public discourse, political debates, and policymaking decisions.
Educating the public about Social Security benefits, program changes, and retirement planning strategies is essential for fostering informed decision-making and public support for policy reforms.
Implications for Retirement Planning:

Policy Uncertainty:

Policy uncertainty surrounding Social Security reforms and legislative changes can create challenges for retirement planning and decision-making.
Individuals must stay informed about proposed policy changes, evaluate their potential impact on retirement benefits, and adapt their retirement plans accordingly.
Long-Term Planning:

Long-term retirement planning requires individuals to consider various policy scenarios, economic conditions, and demographic trends that may impact Social Security benefits and retirement income.
Diversification of retirement income sources, proactive savings strategies, and flexibility in retirement plans can help individuals navigate policy uncertainties and achieve financial security in retirement.
Advocacy and Engagement:

Advocacy efforts and civic engagement play a vital role in shaping public policy and influencing legislative decisions related to Social Security and retirement security.
Individuals, advocacy groups, and stakeholders can advocate for policy reforms, raise awareness about retirement issues, and promote solutions to strengthen Social Security and enhance retirement security for all Americans.

By understanding the broader public affairs and policy considerations surrounding Social Security planning, individuals can navigate the complexities of retirement planning with greater insight and foresight. In the following chapters, we'll continue to explore strategies for Social Security planning, retirement preparation, and achieving financial well-being in later years.

So, let's dive in and explore the dynamic intersection of public affairs and policy with Social Security planning.

Chapter: Debates Surrounding Social Security Reform

Welcome to the chapter dedicated to exploring the debates surrounding Social Security reform. In this chapter, we'll delve into the various viewpoints, proposals, and controversies surrounding efforts to reform the Social Security program. Understanding these debates is essential for individuals planning for retirement and policymakers seeking to ensure the long-term sustainability and adequacy of Social Security benefits.

Social Security reform is a perennial topic of debate among policymakers, economists, advocacy groups, and the general public. As demographic shifts, economic challenges, and fiscal concerns evolve, discussions about the future of Social Security continue to shape public policy and retirement planning strategies.

Key Areas of Debate:

Funding and Solvency:

One of the primary debates surrounding Social Security reform is how to address funding shortfalls and ensure the long-term solvency of the program.
Policymakers propose various reforms, such as adjusting payroll taxes, raising the retirement age, reducing benefits, or increasing revenue streams, to address funding challenges and strengthen the financial stability of Social Security.
Retirement Age:

The debate over the retirement age centers on whether to adjust the Full Retirement Age (FRA) to reflect increases in life expectancy and changes in workforce participation.
Proponents of raising the retirement age argue that it is necessary to align benefits with demographic realities and reduce financial strain on the Social Security system, while opponents raise concerns about the impact on vulnerable populations and those with physically demanding jobs.
Benefit Levels:

Discussions about benefit levels revolve around balancing the need to provide adequate retirement income for beneficiaries while ensuring the long-term sustainability of the Social Security program.
Proposals to adjust benefit formulas, means-test benefits, or index benefits to inflation aim to address concerns about the adequacy of Social Security benefits and the program's fiscal outlook.
Taxation and Revenue:

The debate over taxation and revenue focuses on how to generate sufficient revenue to fund Social Security benefits without unduly burdening taxpayers or undermining economic growth.

Proposals to increase payroll taxes, expand the tax base, or implement alternative revenue sources seek to address funding shortfalls and ensure the financial viability of Social Security for future generations.
Equity and Social Justice:

Discussions about equity and social justice center on how Social Security reforms may impact different demographic groups, income levels, and socioeconomic statuses. Advocates for equity argue for reforms that protect vulnerable populations, mitigate income inequality, and promote intergenerational fairness, while critics raise concerns about unintended consequences and the distributional impact of reform proposals.
Implications for Retirement Planning:

Uncertainty and Planning Challenges:

The ongoing debates surrounding Social Security reform create uncertainty and challenges for retirement planning, as individuals must navigate potential changes to benefit levels, retirement ages, and program parameters.
Long-term retirement planning requires individuals to consider various policy scenarios, adapt to changing legislative landscapes, and incorporate flexibility into their retirement plans.
Advocacy and Engagement:

Advocacy efforts and civic engagement play a vital role in shaping Social Security reform debates and influencing policymakers' decisions.
Individuals, advocacy groups, and stakeholders can engage in advocacy efforts, educate policymakers, and advocate for policy reforms that promote the long-term sustainability and adequacy of Social Security benefits.
Diversification and Flexibility:

Diversification of retirement income sources and flexibility in retirement plans are essential strategies for mitigating the impact of Social Security reform debates on retirement security.

By diversifying retirement savings, exploring alternative income streams, and remaining adaptable to changing policy environments, individuals can enhance their financial resilience and achieve greater retirement security. Navigating the debates surrounding Social Security reform requires individuals to stay informed, engage in advocacy efforts, and adapt their retirement plans to evolving policy landscapes. In the following chapters, we'll continue to explore strategies for Social Security planning, retirement preparation, and achieving financial well-being in later years.

So, let's dive in and explore the complex and dynamic debates surrounding Social Security reform.

Chapter: Advocacy and Community Involvement

Welcome to the chapter dedicated to exploring the importance of advocacy and community involvement in the realm of Social Security planning and retirement security. In this chapter, we'll delve into the role of advocacy, grassroots movements, and community engagement in shaping public policy, raising awareness, and empowering individuals to advocate for their retirement needs and interests.

Advocacy and community involvement are essential components of the democratic process, allowing individuals, organizations, and communities to influence public policy, advocate for social change, and promote the common good. In the context of Social Security planning and retirement security, advocacy efforts play a crucial role in ensuring the adequacy, fairness, and sustainability of Social Security benefits for current and future generations.

Key Aspects of Advocacy and Community Involvement:

Raising Awareness:

Advocacy efforts aim to raise awareness about Social Security issues, retirement challenges, and policy proposals among the general public, policymakers, and stakeholders.

By educating individuals about the importance of Social Security benefits, retirement planning strategies, and advocacy opportunities, advocates can mobilize support for policy reforms and public initiatives.
Policy Engagement:

Advocacy involves engaging with policymakers, elected officials, and government agencies to advocate for policy changes, legislative reforms, and program improvements. Advocates may participate in legislative hearings, submit public comments, meet with policymakers, and advocate for specific policy proposals to address Social Security challenges and enhance retirement security.
Grassroots Organizing:

Grassroots movements and community organizations play a vital role in mobilizing individuals, building coalitions, and amplifying the voices of diverse stakeholders in advocacy efforts.
Grassroots organizers engage community members, host events, and coordinate advocacy campaigns to promote public awareness, civic engagement, and collective action on Social Security and retirement issues.
Coalition Building:

Advocacy efforts often involve coalition building among diverse stakeholders, including retirees, workers, advocacy groups, labor unions, and professional associations. Coalitions leverage collective resources, expertise, and networks to advocate for shared goals, influence policy decisions, and advance the interests of retirees and beneficiaries.
Legislative Action:

Advocacy may lead to legislative action, such as the introduction of bills, resolutions, or amendments aimed at reforming Social Security, protecting retirement benefits, or addressing specific retirement challenges.
Advocates work collaboratively with lawmakers, legislative staff, and advocacy partners to draft legislation, build support, and advocate for passage of bills that promote retirement security and social equity.
Implications for Retirement Planning:

Empowerment and Engagement:

Advocacy and community involvement empower individuals to take an active role in shaping public policy, influencing decision-making, and advocating for their retirement needs and interests.
By engaging in advocacy efforts, individuals can amplify their voices, raise awareness about retirement issues, and advocate for policy reforms that strengthen Social Security and enhance retirement security for all Americans.
Collective Action and Impact:

Collective action through advocacy and community involvement enables individuals to achieve greater impact, effect systemic change, and advance shared goals and priorities.
By joining forces with like-minded advocates, community organizations, and advocacy coalitions, individuals can leverage their collective influence to drive positive change and improve retirement outcomes for themselves and future generations.
Civic Responsibility and Participation:

Advocacy and community involvement reflect a sense of civic responsibility and commitment to promoting social justice, economic equity, and the common good.

By actively participating in advocacy efforts, individuals uphold democratic values, exercise their rights as citizens, and contribute to the collective well-being of society.
Advocacy and community involvement are essential drivers of social change and progress in the realm of Social Security planning and retirement security. By engaging in advocacy efforts, individuals can make meaningful contributions to shaping public policy, protecting retirement benefits, and securing a dignified and prosperous retirement for themselves and future generations.

In the following chapters, we'll continue to explore strategies for Social Security planning, retirement preparation, and achieving financial well-being in later years. Let's continue our journey toward a more secure and equitable retirement future through advocacy and community involvement.

Chapter: Understanding the Future of Social Security

Welcome to the chapter dedicated to exploring the future of Social Security and the challenges and opportunities that lie ahead. In this chapter, we'll delve into the demographic, economic, and policy trends shaping the future of Social Security benefits, retirement planning strategies, and the retirement landscape in the United States.

Social Security is facing a myriad of challenges, including demographic shifts, fiscal pressures, and evolving retirement patterns, that raise questions about the program's long-term sustainability and adequacy. Understanding these challenges is essential for individuals planning for retirement and policymakers seeking to ensure the viability of Social Security for future generations.

Key Trends Shaping the Future of Social Security:

Demographic Shifts:

Demographic changes, such as the aging of the population, declining birth rates, and increased life expectancy, have significant implications for Social Security financing and benefit obligations.
As the baby boomer generation ages into retirement and the ratio of retirees to workers increases, pressure mounts on the Social Security trust funds and the sustainability of benefit payments.
Economic Conditions:

Economic factors, including economic growth, inflation, wage trends, and labor force participation rates, impact Social Security revenues, benefit levels, and program finances. Economic uncertainties, such as recessions, financial crises, and global economic trends, pose challenges to Social Security financing and the ability to maintain benefit adequacy over time.
Policy Reforms:

Policymakers continue to debate and propose reforms to address the long-term solvency of Social Security and ensure the program's financial sustainability.
Reform proposals may include adjustments to benefit formulas, retirement ages, payroll taxes, cost-of-living adjustments (COLA), or program parameters to address funding shortfalls and strengthen the program's fiscal outlook.
Retirement Patterns:

Evolving retirement patterns, such as changes in retirement ages, labor force participation rates, and retirement savings behaviors, impact Social Security benefit claims and program expenditures.
Factors such as increased life expectancy, rising healthcare costs, and shifts in workforce participation may influence individuals' retirement decisions and the timing of Social Security benefit claiming.
Challenges and Opportunities:

Funding Shortfalls:

Social Security faces funding shortfalls due to demographic shifts, economic uncertainties, and policy challenges that threaten the long-term solvency of the program.

Addressing funding shortfalls requires policymakers to enact reforms that enhance revenue streams, control benefit costs, and ensure the financial sustainability of Social Security for future generations.
Benefit Adequacy:

Ensuring the adequacy of Social Security benefits is essential for providing retirees with a reliable source of retirement income that meets their basic needs and maintains their standard of living.
Policymakers must balance competing priorities, such as benefit levels, revenue adequacy, and program affordability, to preserve the adequacy and integrity of Social Security benefits over time.
Retirement Security:

The future of Social Security is closely linked to broader efforts to promote retirement security and financial well-being for individuals and families.
Enhancing retirement security requires a comprehensive approach that integrates Social Security benefits with employer-sponsored retirement plans, personal savings, and other income sources to provide a diversified and sustainable retirement income.
Policy Innovation:

Addressing the future challenges of Social Security requires innovative policy solutions that balance fiscal sustainability with social equity and intergenerational fairness.
Policymakers, advocates, and stakeholders must collaborate to develop creative solutions, promote public dialogue, and build consensus around reforms that strengthen Social Security and enhance retirement security for all Americans.
Implications for Retirement Planning:

Proactive Planning:

Proactive retirement planning is essential for individuals to navigate the uncertainties of Social Security and prepare for future retirement challenges.
Individuals should assess their retirement goals, evaluate their financial resources, and develop strategies to optimize Social Security benefits, supplement retirement income, and achieve long-term financial security.
Flexibility and Adaptability:

Flexibility and adaptability are key principles of retirement planning in an uncertain future, as individuals may need to adjust their plans in response to changing economic conditions, policy reforms, and personal circumstances. Maintaining flexibility in retirement plans allows individuals to respond to unforeseen challenges, seize opportunities, and adapt to evolving retirement landscapes.
Advocacy and Engagement:

Advocacy and community involvement are essential tools for individuals to advocate for their retirement needs, engage with policymakers, and shape the future of Social Security. By actively participating in advocacy efforts, individuals can influence policy decisions, raise awareness about retirement issues, and promote reforms that enhance retirement security for themselves and future generations.
As we look to the future of Social Security, it's clear that proactive planning, innovative policy solutions, and collective action are essential for ensuring the long-term viability and adequacy of Social Security benefits. By understanding the challenges and opportunities ahead, individuals can navigate the complexities of retirement planning with confidence and prepare for a secure and fulfilling retirement.

In the following chapters, we'll continue to explore strategies for Social Security planning, retirement preparation, and achieving financial well-being in later years. Let's embark on this journey together and build a brighter future for retirement security.

Chapter: Conclusion - Recap of Key Takeaways

Congratulations! You've reached the conclusion of our journey through the intricacies of Social Security planning and retirement preparation. In this concluding chapter, let us recap the key takeaways from our exploration and reflect on the essential insights gained along the way.

Importance of Social Security Planning:

Social Security benefits serve as a vital source of retirement income for millions of Americans, providing financial security and stability in retirement.
Understanding Social Security rules, claiming strategies, and benefit options is essential for maximizing retirement income and achieving long-term financial well-being.
Budgeting and Money Management:

Effective budgeting and money management are foundational principles of retirement planning, allowing individuals to allocate resources wisely, manage expenses, and save for retirement.
Creating a budget, managing debt, and saving for the future are critical steps in building financial security and preparing for retirement.
Retirement Planning Strategies:

Retirement planning involves setting goals, evaluating financial resources, and developing strategies to achieve retirement objectives.

By diversifying retirement income sources, optimizing Social Security benefits, and investing in retirement savings accounts, individuals can enhance their retirement security and achieve financial independence.
Social Security Benefits and Claiming Strategies:

Social Security benefits are based on factors such as work history, earnings record, and claiming age, with options to claim benefits as early as age 62 or delay until age 70. Understanding claiming strategies, spousal benefits, survivor benefits, and taxation rules is essential for optimizing Social Security benefits and maximizing retirement income potential.
Healthcare Costs and Retirement Expenses:

Planning for healthcare costs and retirement expenses is a critical aspect of retirement preparation, as healthcare expenses can significantly impact retirement budgets and financial security.
Exploring healthcare options, estimating healthcare costs, and considering long-term care needs are essential steps in retirement planning and ensuring adequate healthcare coverage in retirement.
Advocacy and Community Engagement:

Advocacy and community involvement are powerful tools for influencing public policy, raising awareness about retirement issues, and promoting reforms that enhance retirement security.
By engaging in advocacy efforts, individuals can amplify their voices, advocate for their retirement needs, and contribute to positive change in the realm of Social Security and retirement policy.

As we conclude our journey, remember that retirement planning is a dynamic and ongoing process that requires diligence, flexibility, and adaptability. By incorporating the insights gained from our exploration, individuals can navigate the complexities of retirement planning with confidence and prepare for a secure and fulfilling retirement.

Thank you for joining me on this journey through Social Security planning and retirement preparation. I wish you success in your retirement endeavors and a future filled with financial security, happiness, and fulfillment.

Chapter: Empowering Readers to Take Control of Their Social Security Planning

Welcome to the empowering finale of our journey through Social Security planning. In this chapter, we'll explore how readers can take control of their Social Security planning journey, harnessing the knowledge and insights gained from this book to navigate the complexities of retirement preparation with confidence and clarity.

Knowledge is Power:

Understanding the fundamentals of Social Security, retirement planning strategies, and key considerations empowers readers to make informed decisions about their financial future. By arming themselves with knowledge, readers can confidently navigate the intricacies of Social Security rules, claiming strategies, and retirement income options.
Proactive Planning:

Proactive planning is the cornerstone of successful retirement preparation. Readers can take control of their Social Security planning by setting clear retirement goals, evaluating their financial resources, and developing personalized retirement strategies.
By taking proactive steps to save, invest, and optimize Social Security benefits, readers can enhance their retirement security and achieve their long-term financial objectives.
Maximizing Benefits:

Maximizing Social Security benefits requires careful consideration of claiming strategies, spousal benefits, survivor benefits, and taxation rules. Readers can leverage the insights gained from this book to identify opportunities to maximize their Social Security income potential.

By exploring various claiming options, delaying benefits when appropriate, and coordinating benefits with other retirement income sources, readers can optimize their Social Security benefits and enhance their retirement income security.

Flexibility and Adaptability:

Flexibility and adaptability are essential qualities in retirement planning. Readers should remain open to adjusting their retirement plans in response to changing circumstances, economic conditions, and policy landscapes.

By maintaining flexibility in their retirement plans, readers can adapt to unexpected challenges, seize opportunities, and navigate the uncertainties of retirement with resilience and confidence.

Advocacy and Engagement:

Advocacy and community involvement offer readers a platform to advocate for their retirement needs, raise awareness about retirement issues, and influence public policy.

Readers can engage in advocacy efforts, participate in community organizations, and collaborate with stakeholders to promote reforms that enhance retirement security and protect Social Security benefits for future generations.

Seek Professional Guidance:

While this book provides valuable insights and guidance, readers may benefit from seeking professional advice from financial advisors, retirement planners, or Social Security experts.

Certified professionals can offer personalized recommendations, analyze individual circumstances, and provide tailored strategies to optimize Social Security benefits and achieve retirement goals.

By embracing the principles of knowledge, proactive planning, flexibility, and advocacy, readers can take control of their Social Security planning journey and chart a course towards a secure and fulfilling retirement. Remember, the power to shape your financial future lies in your hands. Seize the opportunity to empower yourself and take control of your retirement destiny.

Thank you for embarking on this journey with me. I wish you success in your Social Security planning endeavors and a future filled with prosperity, happiness, and peace of mind.

Chapter: Encouragement for Continued Financial Education and Action

Congratulations on completing your journey through this book on Social Security planning! As you close this chapter, I encourage you to continue your financial education and take action to secure your financial future. Here's a final word of encouragement to empower you on your path forward:

Lifelong Learning:

Financial education is a lifelong journey. Continue to seek out opportunities to expand your knowledge and deepen your understanding of personal finance, retirement planning, and investment strategies.
Explore books, articles, workshops, online courses, and educational resources to stay informed and up-to-date on the latest trends and developments in finance and retirement planning.
Set Goals and Take Action:

Set clear financial goals and take proactive steps to achieve them. Whether it's saving for retirement, paying off debt, or building an emergency fund, every action you take brings you closer to your objectives.
Break down your goals into manageable tasks and create a plan of action to guide your financial decisions and activities. Consistent effort and discipline are key to making progress toward your financial goals.
Embrace Financial Empowerment:

Take ownership of your financial future and embrace the power of financial empowerment. You have the ability to shape your financial destiny through informed decision-making, responsible money management, and strategic planning.

Empower yourself to make smart financial choices, advocate for your financial interests, and pursue opportunities for growth and prosperity.

Seek Support and Collaboration:

Don't hesitate to seek support and guidance from trusted advisors, mentors, or financial professionals. Surround yourself with a supportive network of individuals who can offer insights, encouragement, and assistance along your financial journey.

Collaborate with family members, friends, or community groups to share resources, exchange ideas, and support each other's financial goals and aspirations.

Celebrate Progress and Stay Motivated:

Celebrate your financial victories, no matter how small, and acknowledge the progress you've made towards your goals. Recognize the effort and dedication you've invested in improving your financial well-being.

Stay motivated by envisioning the future you want to create for yourself and your loved ones. Keep your long-term goals in mind as you navigate the ups and downs of your financial journey.

Remember, financial success is not measured solely by the size of your bank account but by the sense of security, freedom, and fulfillment it brings to your life. By continuing to educate yourself, set goals, take action, and collaborate with others, you can build a brighter financial future and achieve your dreams.

As you embark on the next chapter of your financial journey, carry with you the knowledge, confidence, and determination you've gained from this book. May your path be filled with abundance, prosperity, and joy.

Appendices: Glossary of Social Security Terms

In this glossary, you'll find definitions for key Social Security terms and concepts to help you navigate the complexities of the Social Security system and retirement planning:

Full Retirement Age (FRA):

The age at which individuals are eligible to receive full Social Security retirement benefits. FRA varies based on birth year, ranging from 65 to 67.
Delayed Retirement Credits (DRCs):

Additional credits earned by delaying Social Security benefits beyond full retirement age. DRCs increase the monthly benefit amount for each year of delay up to age 70.
Primary Insurance Amount (PIA):

The monthly benefit amount payable to an individual at full retirement age, based on their earnings history and Social Security contributions.
Cost-of-Living Adjustment (COLA):

An annual adjustment to Social Security benefits to account for increases in the cost of living as measured by the Consumer Price Index for Urban Wage Earners and Clerical Workers (CPI-W).
Earnings Test:

A provision that reduces Social Security benefits for individuals who continue working and earn income above a certain threshold before reaching full retirement age.
Spousal Benefits:

Social Security benefits available to spouses of retired, disabled, or deceased workers, based on the earnings record of the worker. Spousal benefits may be equal to half of the worker's benefit amount.
Survivor Benefits:

Social Security benefits payable to eligible survivors of deceased workers, including spouses, children, and dependent parents, based on the earnings record of the deceased worker.
Disability Benefits:

Social Security benefits available to individuals who are unable to work due to a severe and long-lasting disability, as defined by the Social Security Administration.
Windfall Elimination Provision (WEP):

A provision that reduces Social Security benefits for individuals who receive pensions from employment not covered by Social Security, such as certain government or foreign work.
Government Pension Offset (GPO):

A provision that reduces spousal or survivor benefits for individuals who receive pensions from government employment not covered by Social Security.
Supplemental Security Income (SSI):

A federal income supplement program that provides financial assistance to aged, blind, and disabled individuals with limited income and resources.

Social Security Trust Funds:

Funds maintained by the Social Security Administration to pay Social Security benefits. The trust funds consist of the Old-Age and Survivors Insurance (OASI) Trust Fund and the Disability Insurance (DI) Trust Fund.
This glossary provides a starting point for understanding Social Security terminology and concepts. For more detailed information and personalized guidance, consider consulting the Social Security Administration website or speaking with a financial advisor specializing in retirement planning.

Happy reading and may your newfound knowledge empower you to make informed decisions about your Social Security benefits and retirement planning!

Chapter: Worksheets and Tools for Financial Planning

In this chapter, you'll find a selection of worksheets and tools designed to assist you in your financial planning journey, including retirement planning, budgeting, and Social Security optimization. These resources are designed to help you assess your financial situation, set goals, and develop actionable strategies to achieve financial security and retirement readiness.

Retirement Planning Worksheet:

This worksheet will help you estimate your retirement income needs, assess your current retirement savings, and determine how much you need to save each month to reach your retirement goals. It includes sections for projecting Social Security benefits, employer-sponsored retirement plan contributions, and personal savings contributions.
Budgeting Template:

This budgeting template allows you to track your income, expenses, and savings goals on a monthly basis. It includes categories for fixed expenses (e.g., housing, utilities) and variable expenses (e.g., groceries, entertainment), as well as sections for setting savings targets and tracking progress towards financial goals.
Social Security Optimization Calculator:

This calculator helps you explore different Social Security claiming strategies and estimate the impact of various claiming ages on your lifetime benefits. By inputting your birth year, earnings history, and retirement age, you can compare the cumulative benefits of claiming early, at full retirement age, or delaying benefits until age 70.
Debt Repayment Plan:

This worksheet assists you in creating a debt repayment plan to pay off outstanding debts systematically. It allows you to list your debts, including balances, interest rates, and minimum monthly payments, and prioritize repayment strategies based on the debt snowball or debt avalanche methods.
Emergency Fund Calculator:

This calculator helps you determine the ideal size of your emergency fund based on your monthly expenses, risk tolerance, and financial goals. It considers factors such as job stability, health insurance coverage, and potential unexpected expenses to calculate an appropriate emergency fund target.
Investment Risk Assessment Tool:

This tool helps you assess your risk tolerance and investment preferences to make informed decisions about asset allocation and investment strategies. It guides you through a series of questions to gauge your comfort level with different types of investments and recommend suitable investment options.
Retirement Income Projection:

This worksheet projects your retirement income streams, including Social Security benefits, pension payments, and retirement savings withdrawals, to estimate your retirement income sufficiency. It allows you to adjust assumptions such as retirement age, life expectancy, and investment returns to see the impact on your retirement income.

These worksheets and tools are intended to serve as practical resources to support your financial planning efforts. Whether you're just starting to plan for retirement or seeking to optimize your existing financial strategy, these resources can help you clarify your goals, make informed decisions, and take meaningful steps towards financial security and retirement readiness.

Feel free to customize these worksheets and tools to fit your individual needs and circumstances. Remember, financial planning is a dynamic process, and regular review and adjustment are essential for staying on track towards your financial goals.

Happy planning, and may these resources empower you to build a brighter financial future!